The
Country
Artist

The Country Artist

A Story about Beatrix Potter

by David R. Collins
illustrations by Karen Ritz

A Carolrhoda Creative Minds Book

Carolrhoda Books, Inc./Minneapolis

To Susan, with love and affection

This book is available in two editions:
Library binding by Carolrhoda Books, Inc.,
    a division of Lerner Publishing Group
Soft cover by First Avenue Editions,
    an imprint of Lerner Publishing Group
241 First Avenue North
Minneapolis, MN 55401 U.S.A.

Website address: www.lernerbooks.com

Library of Congress Cataloging-in-Publication Data

Collins, David R.
    The country artist: a story about Beatrix Potter / by David R.
Collins; illustrations by Karen Ritz.
        p.   cm. — (A Carolrhoda creative minds book)
    Summary: A biography of the English author and illustrator who
grew up during the Victorian era and whose detailed drawings of
plants and animals found their way into her famous picture books.
    ISBN 0-87614-344-3 (lib. bdg. : alk. paper)
    ISBN 0-87614-509-8 (pbk. : alk. paper)
    1. Potter, Beatrix, 1866–1943—Biography—Juvenile literature.
2. Authors, English—20th century—Biography—Juvenile literature.
3. Illustrators—Great Britain—Biography—Juvenile literature.
4. Children's stories—Authorship—Juvenile literature. 5. Country
life—Great Britain—Juvenile literature. [1. Potter, Beatrix,
1866–1943. 2. Authors, English. 3. Illustrators.] I. Ritz,
Karen, ill. II. Title. III. Series.
PR6031.O72Z575   1989
823'.912—dc19
[B]   88-27417

Manufactured in the United States of America
    14 15 16 17 18 – MA – 07 06 05 04 03

Table of Contents

Chapter One

By the time she was ten, Beatrix Potter should have been a very unhappy child. She had spent almost her whole life in a nursery bedroom and schoolroom on the third floor of a stone house in London. Not only that—there were bars on the windows! She had no playmates. Even her own parents seldom came to see her. Bertram, her five-year-old brother, went off to school. Not Beatrix. Girls in England a hundred years ago— at least the daughters of wealthy "gentlefolk"— were taught at home by a governess. From the moment she was born on July 28, 1866, Beatrix Potter was a gentle person, in her upbringing as well as her actions.

Master Rupert Potter, Beatrix's father, was a barrister. He could practice law anywhere in England. Yet Mr. Potter chose not to practice law at all. When he worked, it was mainly at a hobby he took seriously—photography. His family fortune gave him that choice. Sometimes he still did some drawing as he had done as a younger man. But often in the morning he climbed into the family carriage and directed the coachman to drive him to his club. There he read newspapers and played cards. Or he visited art exhibitions or the studio of his good friend the painter John Everett Millais. He returned home in late afternoon. After dining with his wife, Mr. Potter went off to bed.

For Mistress Helen Potter, Beatrix's mother and the lady of the house, each day also had its pattern. After her marriage, she seldom made time for her own artwork—watercolor painting. Instead, in the mornings she planned the day's meals with the cook. Then it was time for writing letters, arranging fresh flowers, and doing needlepoint. Sometimes a lady friend would stop by to visit. If not, Mrs. Potter would climb into the carriage and go visiting herself.

Beatrix admired her father and sometimes accompanied him to art museums or to visit the studio of Mr. Millais. But more often she watched her parents leave and return. Surely there were days when she wanted to call out, "May I go too, please?" But that would have been improper. If there was one rule in the Potter home, it was that children must be proper at all times. Proper children were most often "seen but not heard" —except when they were invited to participate in family discussions about art and politics.

Young Beatrix lived by such rules. She kept her face and hands scrubbed, her long dark hair carefully combed and parted. Her frocks were always clean and pressed, her voice quiet and polite.

"How dull!" some might say.

"Doesn't a child need friends and family to do things with?" others might ask.

But Beatrix wasn't like many children. The house servants were her special friends. When she was not reciting rules of behavior or helping Beatrix dress and groom herself, Nurse McKenzie was a wonderful storyteller. She told Scottish tales of witches and fairies, of enchanted forests and glens. Ever since Beatrix was five years old, Miss Hammond, the governess, had shared more with her than book lessons. She helped her to know nature, the beauty of flowers and other plants. There was also Cox, the butler. How he fussed to make the silverware shine and the table napkins stand pointed and straight! Yet this same man gathered a delightful collection of feathered and furred creatures for Beatrix. After Cox plucked them from behind neighborhood shrubs and sheds, they shared the third-floor room of the No. 2 house on Bolton Gardens Square. In their boxes, cages, and jars, they were honored members of Beatrix's unusual family.

Two prize mice enjoyed an apartment in a long rectangular box. Beatrix named them Hunca Munca and Appley Dapply. Cox had caught them in the Potter kitchen downstairs.

The snails in the big round fishbowl had so many offspring that Cox was kept busy carrying baby snails outside to the nearest puddle of water.

A bat family found life pleasant in an open parrot cage. The creatures slept each day away, hanging upside down. At dusk they were ready to swoop and dart through the air, pausing now and then to land on Beatrix's fingers.

Few garden rabbits could be comfortable in a third-floor schoolroom. But Benjamin Bunny was. Perhaps he liked having lettuce and mixed greens served to him on a china plate. Or maybe it was the warmth of the hearthrug in front of a crackling fire that pleased Benjamin.

Mrs. Potter surely would have fainted if she had known a hedgehog was sharing her daughter's

bedroom. Yet Tiggy displayed good manners, sipping milk from one of Beatrix's fine teacups.

Yes, Beatrix Potter did have a special family. They were not all present at once, however. The cast of characters in the third-floor room changed constantly. Whenever Beatrix seemed lonely, Cox would appear with a new creature. Whatever he brought back delighted her. It was a new friend to be cared for and loved. It was a welcome visitor to be fed and cleaned. It was also a new subject to draw.

"I think you were born with a pencil in one hand and a sketch pad in the other!" Miss Hammond often said. Beatrix would smile, adding the latest drawing of Hunca Munca or Benjamin Bunny to an ever-growing pile of sketches. She loved watching her roommates. Then she would draw them in their favorite poses. For each portrait Beatrix would make up a story. She could hardly wait to share them with Miss Hammond after her daily lessons.

Beatrix also loved to study paintings and drawings in books. Noticing this and her artistic talent, her parents made sure that the schoolroom was well supplied with new picture books.

As far back as she could remember, Beatrix

had looked forward to summertime. For many years, the Potter family had rented country houses in Scotland. Beatrix delighted in those months of open sky and fresh air. Country folk always seemed to smile and greet her. It did not matter that Bertram, her companion, was five years younger than Beatrix. Together they shared the joy of being away from the London walls that closed them in. They watched frogs hopping along the shores of ponds. They climbed hillsides, sometimes discovering caves. They explored woods and glens.

Often a country path led to fields of purple heather and wildflowers that seemed so much brighter than the tiny squares of blossoms at Bolton Gardens. To Beatrix, who loved drawing flowers as much as she loved drawing animals, nature was a paradise. There was no yellow as bright as snapdragon, no pink as soft as foxglove, no blue as rich as royal larkspur. She sketched and then painted them all.

And in the country there were ducklings to feed. How funny they looked as they waddled to dinner! How eagerly their bills snipped at crumbs! Beatrix rapidly sketched and painted them too. Just for fun, she sometimes drew a proud rabbit walking upright and carrying an umbrella. Another rabbit wore a thick scarf, and still another a fine bonnet—like the scarf and bonnet of Mr. and Mrs. Potter!

Summer was never long enough. Beatrix dreaded returning to Bolton Gardens. She always brought back friends: a frog, beetles, caterpillars, minnows, a bird whose wing needed mending. Following her example, Bertram collected creatures of his own, and Beatrix knew she would inherit his Scottish animal and insect companions when he returned to school.

As summer became autumn, and one year passed into another, Beatrix sometimes wondered about her future. Would she spend her entire life at Bolton Gardens? Surely there was a life beyond the walls that confined her each day. Perhaps there were even more glorious places than the flowered hills of Scotland.

Yet how does one choose what to do in the years ahead? As Beatrix gazed from her third-story window, her future appeared as indistinct as the shapes in the fog settling around the Potter house. Try as she might, Beatrix could not even see the house across the square.

Chapter Two

Life at the house in London was much like the grandfather clock that stood in the front hallway. Each day ticked by predictably, never missing a tock.

Meals arrived for Beatrix at eight in the morning, one in the afternoon, and six in the evening. Each meal was brought to the nursery bedroom by a house servant. Beatrix's father and mother dined in the drawing room. The maids, butler, and coachman ate in the kitchen. By the time she was eleven, Beatrix was convinced she had eaten two million soft-boiled eggs, a million veal cutlets, and a mountain of rice pudding. How she longed for more gingersnap cookies!

Actually it was not the taste of gingersnap

cookies that Beatrix liked best. It was from where they came. Gingersnap cookies were personally delivered by Beatrix's grandmother, known to English society as Mrs. Edmund Crompton Potter.

But Grandmama Potter did not come often to No. 2 Bolton Gardens. She seldom left her yellow brick country house near Hatfield. When she *did* come, it was a special treat. To Beatrix, Grandmama Potter was like those wonderful people in Nurse McKenzie's stories.

Grandmama always looked the same. A white shawl draped over the shoulders of her black silk dress. A nest of gray hair lay carefully bunned under her white lace cap with black velvet ribbons. Her full rosy cheeks were framed by corkscrew ringlets. An unkind stranger might have said her pointed nose looked like a beak. But Beatrix loved Grandmama's sparkling brown eyes and her smile.

Tucked inside Grandmama's hand purse was Piglette. A stuffed doll of white flannel, it had once belonged to Beatrix's father. Try as she might, Beatrix could not imagine her father as a short person without whiskers, clutching Piglette.

"Oh, but he did!" Grandmama would insist, ignoring her son's reddened face.

Piglette and Totsy, Beatrix's favorite doll, got along beautifully. As a younger child, Beatrix had often entertained the two dolls under a table, hidden by a long tablecloth, while the grown-ups chattered nearby. Piglette and Totsy had made good puppets, whispering and nodding in Beatrix's hands as they imitated the grown-ups in the room!

At twelve Beatrix was assigned a chair to sit in during Grandmama's visits. She often brought paper and pencil to record in code what the grown-ups said. Only Beatrix knew the code. Its secret alphabet gave her a way to write down her true thoughts without worrying that someone— especially her mother—would discover them.

Some of what Beatrix recorded was family history—Grandmama Potter's favorite topic. Oh, she was proud to be a Potter. She had married a man who made fortunes, lost them, and made them again. And she was just as proud to be a Crompton. She was fond of mentioning her Crompton ancestors, rebels who had fought against unfair laws. Grandmama spoke of Crompton courage and those who worked to make life better for others. She scolded her son. He was wasting his time at his club, she said. Beatrix listened as she sat in her chair.

"My bills are paid," Rupert Potter answered. "My house is in order."

That was not enough for Grandmama Potter. There was more to life than paying bills and keeping one's house in order, she insisted. One had to make the most of every opportunity. The head of a household had to make certain his children had opportunities too.

"My children lack nothing," Mr. Potter declared.

Grandmama was not so sure. She turned to Bertram and Beatrix. Without words, her face asked them: "Is there anything you want or need?"

Bertram squirmed, stealing a quick look at his father. It was a scary moment for a seven-year-old. He looked down and shook his head.

Beatrix knew how her brother felt. It would be improper to complain. Yet there was something she *did* want—and here was her opportunity to ask for it.

"I...I..." Beatrix hesitated, wiping her nervous hands on her frock. "I think I should like to take drawing lessons."

There. It was done. Her head still bowed, Beatrix was surprised to hear her father consent! Bertram was impressed. Grandmama sat back in her chair. The old woman smiled, happy to know that her granddaughter had some of the Crompton family courage.

But Rupert Potter was determined to have the final word. He turned to look at Bertram. "But you will notice, Mother, that the *boy* is perfectly satisfied. And, after all, is it not more important that a young man receive the benefits of education and position? Surely we know that, of the two children seated here, it is Bertram who will make the greater contribution to our world!"

A knot tugged in Beatrix's stomach. Her gaze met Bertram's. His eyes glistened with apology. How he wished he could stand up and defend his sister! Beatrix could read it in his face. But to speak against their father? He wouldn't dare.

"You might discuss your feelings with our beloved monarch!" Grandmama snapped, rising to her feet. "She should be told that it is only men who make worthy contributions to our world!"

Beatrix's thoughts spun. Of course, "our beloved monarch" meant Queen Victoria. Only today Miss Hammond had spoken of her in their history lesson. Since 1837 Queen Victoria had ruled the British Empire. Now it was 1878. That was forty-one years! Many people thought Queen Victoria was the greatest leader in the world—perhaps in all history. Was Grandmama making fun of her son's thoughts about women? Yes. Beatrix caught the fiery twinkle in the old woman's eyes as she turned to leave.

At that moment Beatrix was convinced there was no greater queen anywhere than the grand lady in black silk who was sweeping through the parlor doorway.

Chapter Three

Mr. Potter kept his promise. Within a week Miss Caroline Cameron presented herself at No. 2 Bolton Gardens. Beatrix discovered her new art teacher had definite ideas about drawing.

"Never trace a picture, putting your own paper over it and drawing," Miss Cameron instructed. Beatrix frowned. She had always enjoyed tracing as well as freehand drawing. Sensing her new student's dismay, Miss Cameron softened. "Never take another person's work," she explained. "You may study it, examine it closely, but never trace it. Draw what *you* see and what *you* feel. Then your artwork will be your own. It will bring you joy."

Beatrix was willing to try. Each day she sketched

flowers in the house. She enjoyed drawing leaf designs too. A chair appeared on her drawing pad, then a table.

Miss Hammond helped. She and Beatrix went for walks, looking for a cluster of wild roses or Canterbury bells. Beatrix found new excitement in her drawing. She no longer liked tracing; she could capture details on her own!

"Look at these mushrooms," the pupil told her instructor. "They look like small umbrellas!"

Miss Cameron nodded and smiled. She knew Beatrix was taking a big step forward in her art studies. There was new life in her work, fresh feeling and imagination.

Bertram shared his sister's interest in drawing. Yet he lacked her patience. After sketching for a few minutes, he wanted more activity. He liked to race around with his microscope and find little items to inspect. Beatrix liked using the microscope too. It helped her see the smallest details of leaves. She drew every tiny vein.

But still Beatrix enjoyed sketching animals the most: rabbits, squirrels, and Tiggy, the hedgehog. She filled a whole notebook with Tiggy drawings. She recorded him in pictures as he ate, slept, and played.

Miss Cameron praised her student's work. Even Mr. Potter approved of what he saw.

But Mrs. Potter simply shook her head. A well-bred girl of thirteen drawing rabbits, squirrels, and a hedgehog? Hardly proper! Why, Beatrix scarcely knew how to play the piano! She could sketch flowers—that much was fitting for a young lady—but she knew little about arranging them. No, Mrs. Potter could only shake her head.

Beatrix's world grew larger. Her walks with Miss Hammond often led to a science museum or an art gallery. Sometimes they went by carriage. For hours Beatrix sketched and studied animals, from their bone structures to the tips of their whiskers. She drew butterflies, beetles, and spiders. In the art galleries, she noted each color and paintbrush stroke used by the great artists. She found herself dreaming of a Beatrix Potter painting hanging on the gallery wall. How grand it would be to have people admiring her creations. What joy it would be to bring pleasure to a stranger's life. Wouldn't Grandmama Potter be proud!

As months and years passed, several people who had brightened Beatrix's days at Bolton Gardens said farewell.

McKenzie was the first to depart, to live her

final years in Scotland. "I'm not sure whether I've helped to raise two children or two zoo-keepers," the old woman mumbled. "Never heard of such a thing—bats and mice and a hedgehog."

Then it was Cox who left, persuaded by a brother to live in America. With a final bow, the gentle butler drew Beatrix into his arms for a farewell hug. "I shall miss you and your little friends," he said. "I never did tell your mum . . . ."

Beatrix smiled, fighting back tears. "I know. Thank you."

Cox shook his head. "Oh, it wasn't for you I kept silent," he said playfully. "It was for your mum. I'm afraid she couldn't have stood the shock!"

Finally even Miss Hammond said good-bye. Beatrix was sixteen, and the kind governess had taught her all she could. Another governess would come to offer lessons in French and German. The parting was especially sad for Beatrix. What would she do without Miss Hammond? She had learned so much from her, in history and science and all the other subjects. But there would be more for her to learn about being a lady, Miss Hammond assured her—there would be new ideas and challenges to explore with the new governess, and on her own.

It was quieter now in the house at Bolton Gardens. With so many of her human friends gone, Beatrix devoted more time to her animal companions. Hunca Munca, Appley Dapply, Benjamin Bunny, lizards, mice, and squirrels all received special care. In a diary Beatrix kept a careful record in code of what each creature did each day.

Yet her third-floor quarters seemed lonely. Beatrix continued her visits to the Kensington Museum by herself. She made friends with a museum clerk named Katie Woodward, a friend of Miss Hammond whose father was a magazine editor. Miss Woodward encouraged Beatrix in her drawing and painting, claiming her artwork was "every bit as professional" as that which appeared in her father's magazine.

During the summer months—which the Potters began to spend in the English Lake District— Beatrix also received encouragement from an old friend of her father, a clergyman and author who lived there. Canon H. D. Rawnsley, the Vicar of Wray, always wore a black suit and a faceful of whiskers. He welcomed Beatrix on his daily walks, and they had long talks in his book-lined study. He shared her love of animals, knowing

every bone and muscle of the creatures who thrived in the dales, near the lakes, or on the hillsides. Someday, he predicted, Beatrix would be known as a "teller of animal tales."

That prediction took a step toward coming true when Miss Annie Carter arrived at the house in London. The new foreign-language instructor was only twenty, while Beatrix was seventeen. Miss Carter had traveled abroad and seemed to know so much about life. She was tall and slender, walked with a spring in her step, and was cheerful and amusing. Mr. Potter wondered how learning could take place with so much laughter, so many giggles between this teacher and his daughter. Once a week he listened to Beatrix recite her lessons. It seemed not to matter to Mr. Potter that he understood neither French nor German.

"Adequate," he would declare after her performance. "Quite adequate."

For two years Beatrix studied, worked, and laughed with Annie. When Annie announced one day that she was getting married and would be moving away, Beatrix was surprised. Like herself, Annie seemed too young to make such a decision. Yet, in many ways, she knew much more of life in the outside world than Beatrix did.

Annie departed, but she made Beatrix promise to visit. Beatrix couldn't have known then that her promise would lead to events that would affect millions of people.

Chapter Four

"Oh, I look dreadful!"

Beatrix hid the mirror under her pillow. For weeks she had suffered rheumatic fever and dizziness. Now her hair was falling out in patches! Bertram was off to college, leaving her lonely and depressed. Only the cheery notes from Annie —now Mrs. William Moore—seemed to spill sunshine into her gloomy bedroom. Beatrix could hear Annie's laughter in each letter. How she longed to make the ten-mile journey to Wandsworth to visit her friend and former teacher!

Mr. and Mrs. Potter were not eager to bid their daughter farewell, even for a short time. They still thought of Beatrix as a child, although she was nearly twenty. Mr. and Mrs. Potter wanted to keep Beatrix under their watchful eye.

As for their son, Bertram had never been the

student they had hoped he might be. So far his leadership had been limited to causing mischief in the schools he attended. His decision to become an artist was an additional worry to his parents, although it delighted Beatrix.

When Beatrix was finally allowed to travel to Wandsworth, the ten-mile trip was like a journey to another world. The door of Annie and William Moore's home opened to the aromas of baking bread and hot cider. Beatrix was welcomed with kisses and hugs from Annie and William's many relatives and friends. There was no guest treatment for Beatrix—she was one of the family. This home was filled with love, a love that chased away loneliness. Beatrix's one-day visits often stretched to two days. It was hard to leave the wonderful world of Wandsworth.

As she slipped into her twenties, Beatrix hoped for more freedom at home. It did not come. Now and then her father still invited her to visit a museum. Her mother took her along on visits to her wealthy London friends once a month. But rarely did anyone ask Beatrix's thoughts or opinions. She felt like an onlooker. Only in her journals did she share her feelings. Her secret code continued to fill page after page.

Beatrix drew as much as she wrote. Rabbits and hedgehogs leapt from her watercolor brush onto paper. Each creature begged for a name, and for each Beatrix made up a story.

When Bertram finished school, he began to earn a living as an artist. His parents were surprised and delighted. Beatrix looked forward to her brother's visits home. He encouraged her to send some of her drawings to publishers. "They are too good not to share," Bertram insisted.

Beatrix was certain her father would disapprove of Bertram's suggestion. A young man might deal with businessmen, but a young woman? Unseemly! For his own daughter to do so—most improper!

Yet, more and more often, Beatrix was showing courage. Never had she taken her animal friends along on summer vacations to Scotland or the Lake District. Now she did. She even shared her stories about her pet roommates with her father and mother, enjoying their astonishment. She went to Wandsworth as often as she wished, sometimes staying for several days. At last, with a new sense of freedom, she packaged up several animal drawings and mailed them off to a publisher.

Back her drawings came.

But with Bertram's coaxing, Beatrix sent them

off again. The second publisher expressed interest, and then invited her for a visit. She went secretly, but was disappointed. The publisher wanted her to draw only what *he* wished. He saw only lines and colors on paper, only the details of what she had drawn and painted. He failed to see the fun and spirit of her work. In her journal she tried to make herself feel better.

"He did not strike me as being a person of much taste," she wrote.

Discouraged but determined, Beatrix again mailed off a number of sketches. This time, in response, she received a check in the mail—and an invitation to illustrate a poetry book.

The first published work of Beatrix Potter appeared during the Christmas holiday of 1890, when Beatrix was twenty-four. Her cheerful drawings of Benjamin Bunny matched the light, humorous verse of the poet Frederic Weatherby. The collection was called *The Happy Pair*. It quickly won its way into the hearts and homes of many English children. In fact it was better received by strangers than by Beatrix's own parents.

"Women do not belong in business!" blustered Mr. Potter.

"Such a thing is hardly suitable for a woman of your position!" Mrs. Potter insisted.

Their criticism hurt. For a time Beatrix did little drawing and writing. She escaped to Wandsworth whenever she could, enjoying the children of her friends Annie and William. But when five-year-old Noel became ill, Beatrix could not visit him in person. So she decided to put pen to paper instead.

> My dear Noel—
> I don't know what to write to you, so I shall tell you a story about four little rabbits whose names were Flopsy, Mopsy, Cottontail and Peter. They lived with their mother in a sandbank . . .

On the story went, of how Flopsy, Mopsy, and Cottontail—but not Peter—followed their mother's orders. Naughty Peter headed right for where he had been told not to go—to mean Mr. McGregor's garden.

Noel was thrilled with the story. "He is one big smile," Annie wrote to Beatrix. "How the other children envy him."

Envy? Beatrix would have none of that!

Soon all of the Moore children had their own

tales. Eric squealed with delight over Little Pig Robinson; Norah treasured the adventures of Squirrel Nutkin. For the youngest child, Freda, Beatrix fashioned a story about the poor tailor of Gloucester, some good, clever mice, and a gentleman's coat. Annie put each letter carefully away. When one of her children was sad, out came a story. Again they would smile at the words and pictures.

Whenever Beatrix would visit, Noel brought out the Peter Rabbit letter. His enthusiasm gave Beatrix a new thought. Maybe other children would enjoy it too. She borrowed the letter and recopied it into a notebook. Then she added more drawings. She began sending it to publishers, one after another.

Back the story came. Rejected. "Regrettably, Madam, we cannot publish your work...," she read. Six more times she sent it out. Only one publisher, Frederick Warne & Company, offered encouragement. Still, the editors turned it down.

"Then, I shall print it myself!" Beatrix declared.

Beatrix had carefully saved her money all her life. Birthday gifts, small allowances, family inheritances—each had gone into her savings account. Now she took out most of the money to cover the cost of printing 250 copies of *The Tale of Peter Rabbit*. The book version was slightly longer than Noel's letter had been, and all the illustrations were in black and white—all but one. Beatrix could not resist paying extra for a color illustration of Mrs. Bunny giving disobedient Peter a dose of camomile tea. Its brightness added something special to the slim volume.

Beatrix marched boldly into a neighborhood bookstore and persuaded the owner to sell her book. The bookstore sold its copies quickly, and the owner asked for more. Everyone seemed to enjoy the story. Even Mr. and Mrs. Potter seemed a bit proud of what their daughter had done. Before Beatrix had time to get more books printed, a letter arrived from Frederick Warne & Company. People at the publishing house had seen her book. If she was willing to make *all* color illustrations for it, they would publish it themselves! Beatrix was delighted.

In 1902 *The Tale of Peter Rabbit* was published by Frederick Warne & Company. Beatrix was thirty-six years old.

The publisher's son, Norman Warne, began to take a personal interest in Beatrix. Norman invited her to meet his family. His mother was a widow who lived with him and his sister, Millie, in a big house on Bedford Square in London. The Warne home always seemed warm and cheerful, especially when the two married Warne brothers brought their families to visit. It reminded Beatrix of the Moore home in Wandsworth.

Norman asked Beatrix if she had other stories like *The Tale of Peter Rabbit*. Fortunately Annie Moore still kept the letters that Beatrix had written to the children. Norman persuaded Beatrix to let Frederick Warne & Company publish the stories in the letters, with their colorful pictures, as new books. *The Tailor of Gloucester* became a quick success. By the time *The Tale of Squirrel Nutkin* appeared, the name of Beatrix Potter was known to any child in England under the age of ten. Letters poured in from her fans.

"You are the goodest mum to ever put pen on paper," wrote one child.

"May your bunnies and squirrels live forever!" wrote another.

Never had Beatrix been so happy. Her mind filled with more stories and pictures. But in her heart there was also room for Norman Warne. He became more than a kind editor. He became a

good friend—a best friend. They went on picnics, long walks, and carriage rides. Even when they did nothing at all, they enjoyed being together. When Norman asked her to marry him, Beatrix agreed.

It was not a decision that pleased her parents. They strongly objected. After all, Norman Warne was a tradesperson, a common working man.

Beatrix was nearly forty years old. She loved the Warne family. Already Norman's nieces and nephews called her "Auntie Bee." Yes, despite her parents, she would marry Norman Warne. She would put the gloomy days of Bolton Gardens behind her.

But it was not to be. During the summer of 1905, Norman became ill with leukemia. At the end of August, he died.

The Warne family tried to comfort Beatrix. Norman's sister, Millie, was especially helpful. She encouraged Beatrix to keep working. "It is what Norman would have wanted," Millie said.

Beatrix knew Millie was right. Yet, without Norman, her life would never be quite the same. For a long time, the creatures in Beatrix's sketches seemed to have sad faces.

Chapter Five

During the years that followed, Beatrix found herself remembering past summers in the country that had made her feel happy and free. Sheep and cattle grazing in the pastures, sparkling brooks, and meadows of wildflowers all gave her special joy. When a small farm in the Lake District came up for sale in 1906, Beatrix bought it. She was proud that she had earned the money to buy it herself from the sales of her books.

It was called Hill Top Farm. The main house was a small gray cottage that looked as though it had sprouted out of the hill it sat upon. Climbing vines laced the outside walls. Roses and lilacs grew wild in the surrounding garden. Inside there were small rooms and a big kitchen that had never had electricity.

"It is my heaven," Beatrix wrote to Millie Warne.

Hill Top Farm offered an escape from No. 2 Bolton Gardens. Whenever she could, Beatrix fled from the dreariness of London to the fresh open country. The creatures of Hill Top inspired her to create many new story characters. Rats seemed to think the cottage belonged to them, and their story came to life in *The Roly-Poly Pudding*. Beatrix portrayed a friendlier acquaintance in *The Tale of Jemima Puddle-Duck*. Readers visited her garden in *The Tale of Tom Kitten* and *The Tale of Pigling Bland*.

Brother Bertram tried to persuade Beatrix to move to Scotland where he now lived. He still drew and painted, but he was a farmer too. Although she appreciated his invitation, Beatrix declined. England was her home. She still felt an obligation to look after Mr. and Mrs. Potter in their later years.

But Beatrix spent time at Hill Top Farm whenever she could. A farmer, John Cannon, stayed there with his family, taking care of things while Beatrix was in London. She had him build special living quarters for himself and his family, a small library for her books and Bertram's paintings, and a dairy.

The animal family at Hill Top grew. Sheep,

pigs, cows, and chickens all lived there. John Cannon taught Beatrix about raising livestock. Before long she was showing prize sheep in local fairs. "That ram obeys you as if you were his mother," one sheep judge remarked. Beatrix smiled. A mother was exactly what she felt like!

As Beatrix spent more and more time on the farm, she spent less and less time writing and drawing. There was always a fence to have fixed or a bush to prune. She loved to walk to the village of Sawrey nearby and often returned with garden plants that friendly neighbors had given her to plant at Hill Top.

Yet, when she *did* create, Beatrix depicted the world that was her delight. Ten new books—in nine years—grew out of her life in the country. In them Hill Top Farm appeared often, with its cupboards and attics, its hiding spots in the garden, its lively farmyard of gossiping animal neighbors.

"A writer should use what [she] knows and feels," Beatrix wrote to Millie. "I suppose I shall always be a child. I am afraid my parents would frown on me for making such a statement. Yet perhaps there are a few of the younger set who will understand me. It is for them I write and sketch. I hope I can bring them pleasure."

There was little doubt of that. Children everywhere begged their parents for another reading of the tales of Mr. Jeremy Fisher, the Flopsy Bunnies, or Mrs. Tittlemouse. Each book by Beatrix Potter was an instant success.

As the new books appeared, the earlier titles spread to more bookstores and libraries. Peter Rabbit quickly became a favorite of young readers in France, Germany, and Spain. Beatrix's first story was translated into more and more languages so that children far from England could learn of Peter's adventure. Although the words were different in other languages, the story remained the same and was loved everywhere. The book was brought to America and published there by people who paid Beatrix nothing for the story, but it pleased her to know that American boys and girls welcomed Peter too.

In 1909 Beatrix learned that Castle Cottage Farm next to Hill Top was for sale. She could use more space for livestock and farming, so she contacted Mr. William Heelis—the man hired by the owner to sell it. Not only was he helpful with the sale, he helped lay the water pipe to Beatrix's new land. He shared her love for the country. Soon he began to visit Hill Top often, not just on business, but because he was beginning to care about Beatrix herself.

Before she could enjoy Castle Cottage Farm, Beatrix became ill. Fever and dizziness kept her in bed, and finally her parents insisted she return to Bolton Gardens so they could look after her. They scolded her for working too hard on her writing and on the farm.

Too tired and sick to argue, Beatrix returned to London. She soon realized that the brightest moment of each day at Bolton Gardens came with the arrival of the afternoon mail. She almost leapt from her bed as the servant carried in the daily letters. William Heelis wrote often, and for Beatrix his words were better than any medicine. How she missed their long talks and walks! Her desire to be with him sped her recovery.

Soon after her return to Hill Top Farm, William proposed to Beatrix. Once again she knew her parents would not approve. They would not think William Heelis was rich enough or important enough to join the Potter family.

Beatrix was right.

During one of her next stays in London, Bertram came to visit. He could not have come at a better time. He openly approved of Beatrix's

desire to marry a working man. Not only that—Bertram announced to his parents that he had been married for eleven years!

"But you never told us!" Mrs. Potter gasped.

Bertram shook his head. He explained that his wife's father was a small shopkeeper in Scotland. His was hardly a marriage of which the proud Potters would have approved.

Bertram's announcement was just the support that Beatrix needed. On October 14, 1913, she became Mrs. William Heelis. She was forty-seven years old. The newlywed couple moved to Castle Cottage Farm.

With a husband who shared her love for the country, Beatrix could meet the future with new hope. She put the loneliness and gloom of No. 2 Bolton Gardens behind her.

But, sadly, most of Beatrix's writing and drawing days were also in the past. Her eyesight had weakened, and she preferred working outside in the garden or with her animals.

Visitors came to the Sawrey countryside, hoping to see or meet Beatrix. By now she was famous. Yet she had no wish to open her quiet life to strangers. A smile or a wave was all she would offer.

More and more Beatrix blended into the rustic

countryside. She became a good cook, her own plump figure revealing her success. No longer did she wear the clothes of a middle-aged spinster raised among gentlefolk. She wore old sweaters and tweed skirts. On her head she wore straw hats; on her feet, loose wooden clogs.

"Oh, no, that couldn't be Miss Beatrix Potter!" more than one visitor remarked. "That's just a common country farm wife!"

Such comments amused Beatrix. She felt like a part of nature, and it was a feeling she relished.

Few events in the outside world disturbed the quiet of the Lake District. World War I, the Great Depression, the death of King George V, the giving up of the crown by King Edward VIII, the crowning of King George VI—like her neighbors, Beatrix learned of such news. But the Sawrey countryside was a world unto itself. Its residents lived from day to day, removed from events beyond the hills.

Children who grew up reading about Peter Rabbit and his friends became mothers and fathers who read the stories to their own children. Now and then a new book by Beatrix Potter appeared and was eagerly welcomed by fans around the world. She used the money from her books to buy more farms and land, renting out her properties to others.

"I wish other people might know this world of the country," Beatrix wrote to Millie Warne. "It is such a pure and simple life. Time has forgotten us and we are grateful."

Beatrix's wish for others to experience nature encouraged her to read about the British National Trust. Canon Rawnsley, her old friend, had helped to start it. It was an organization that bought land and protected it from modern changes. Birds and other animals could live on this land without fear, and its lakes and hills would remain clear of resorts and highways. Now in her seventies, Beatrix made arrangements to turn her land and farms over to the National Trust after her death. William supported her plan.

During World War II and the German bombing of London, Beatrix learned that the Potter house at No. 2 Bolton Gardens Square had been destroyed. It was as though the final chapter of her family history had been finished. Mr. Potter had died in 1914, Bertram in 1918, and Mrs. Potter in 1932. Now the old home was also gone.

One evening, from their farmhouse window, Beatrix and William watched the sky glow with distant bombs and fires. Beatrix remarked that she could almost hear people crying—the ugliness of war had finally invaded the peace of the English countryside.

On December 22, 1943, Beatrix Potter died at Castle Cottage Farm. She was seventy-seven years old. Her farms and land, over 4000 acres, were turned over to the National Trust. Visitors today can enjoy Hill Top Farm almost as Beatrix did, for it has been kept up without changes. Not surprisingly, rabbits seem to be peering from behind every tree and bush.

The real gift of Beatrix Potter, though, was the fun and fantasy she offered to children everywhere. Peter Rabbit and his friends live on around the world.

BOOKLIST

Beatrix Potter's books for children are available in bookstores and libraries:

The Tale of Peter Rabbit
The Tailor of Gloucester
The Tale of Squirrel Nutkin
The Tale of Benjamin Bunny
The Tale of Two Bad Mice
The Tale of Mrs. Tiggy-Winkle
The Pie and the Patty-Pan
The Tale of Mr. Jeremy Fisher
The Story of a Fierce Bad Rabbit
The Story of Miss Moppet
The Tale of Tom Kitten
The Tale of Jemima Puddle-Duck
The Tale of the Roly-Poly Pudding
The Tale of the Flopsy Bunnies

Ginger and Pickles

The Tale of Mrs. Tittlemouse

The Tale of Timmy Tiptoes

The Tale of Mr. Tod

The Tale of Pigling Bland

Appley Dapply's Nursery Rhymes

The Tale of Johnny Townmouse

Cecily Parsley's Nursery Rhymes

The Fairy Caravan

The Tale of Little Pig Robinson

Wag-by-Wall

The Tale of the Faithful Dove

The Sly Old Cat

The Tale of Tuppenny (illustrated by
Marie Angel)

BIBLIOGRAPHY

Aldis, Dorothy. *Nothing is Impossible.* New York: Antheneum, 1969.

Lane, Margaret. *The Magic Years of Beatrix Potter.* London: Frederick Warne & Co. Ltd., 1978.

Lane, Margaret. *The Tale of Beatrix Potter.* London: Frederick Warne & Co. Ltd., 1946.

Linder, Leslie. *A History of the Writings of Beatrix Potter.* London: Frederick Warne & Co. Ltd., 1971.

Mayer, Ann Margaret. *The Two Worlds of Beatrix Potter.* Mankato, Minnesota: Creative Education, 1974.

Taylor, Judy. *Beatrix Potter: Artist, Storyteller & Countrywoman,* London: Frederick Warne & Co. Ltd., 1987.

HENRY

JAMES

PERCY

TITLES AVAILABLE IN BUZZ BOOKS

First published 1990 by Buzz Books,
an imprint of the Octopus Publishing Group.
Michelin House, 81 Fulham Road, London SW3 6RB

LONDON MELBOURNE AUCKLAND

Copyright © William Heinemann Ltd 1990

All publishing rights: William Heinemann Ltd. All television
and merchandising rights licensed by William Heinemann Ltd
to Britt Allcroft (Thomas) Ltd exclusively, worldwide.

Photographs © Britt Allcroft (Thomas) Ltd 1985, 1986
Photographs by David Mitton, Kenny McArthur and
Terry Permane for Britt Allcroft's production of
Thomas the Tank Engine and Friends.

ISBN 1 85591 025 X

Printed and bound in the UK by BPCC Paulton Books Ltd.

THOMAS
AND TERENCE

buzz books

Autumn had come to the Island of Sodor.
The leaves were changing from green to
brown. The fields were changing too, from
yellow stubble to brown earth.

As Thomas puffed along on his branch
line with Annie and Clarabel, he heard the
"chug chug chug" of a tractor at work.

One day, stopping for a signal, he saw the tractor close by.

"Hullo!" said the tractor. "I'm Terence; I'm ploughing."

"Hullo!" said Thomas. "I'm Thomas; I'm pulling a train. What *ugly* wheels you've got."

Terence said that his wheels were not
ugly.

"They're caterpillars!" he said. "I can go
anywhere; *I* don't need rails."

"I don't want to go *anywhere*," said
Thomas, huffily. "I like my rails, thank you."

Soon winter came with dark heavy clouds, full of snow. Thomas's driver didn't like it.

"A heavy fall is coming," he said. "I hope it doesn't stop us."

"Pooh!" said Thomas. "Snow is silly soft stuff, nothing to it!" And he puffed on, taking no notice.

Thomas finished his journey safely, but by now the fields were covered and the rails were two dark lines standing out in the white snow.

"You'll need your snow plough for the next journey, Thomas," said his driver.

"Pooh! Snow is silly soft stuff – it won't stop me!" Thomas snorted.

"Listen to me," said his driver. "We are going to put this snow plough on and I want no nonsense, please!"

The snow plough was heavy and uncomfortable and made Thomas cross. He shook it and banged it and when they got back it was so damaged that the driver had to take it off.

"You're a very naughty engine," the driver said, as he closed the shed door that night.

Next morning, Thomas's driver and fireman arrived early and worked hard to mend the snow plough, but they couldn't fix it.

Soon it was time for the first train. Thomas was pleased.

"I shan't have to wear it! I shan't have to wear it!" he puffed.

"I hope it's all right. I hope it's all right," Annie and Clarabel whispered to each other.

The driver was worried too.

"The snow's not bad here," he said to the fireman, "but it's sure to be deep in the valley."

It had been snowing again. Thomas started with his train full of passengers.

"Silly soft stuff! Silly soft stuff!" he puffed. "I didn't need that stupid old thing yesterday and I shan't need it today. Snow can't stop *me*."

Thomas rushed into the tunnel, thinking how clever he was. But there was trouble ahead.

At the other end of the tunnel he could see that a heap of snow had fallen from the sides of the cutting.

"Silly soft stuff!" said Thomas and he charged into the snow. "Cinders and ashes!" he cried. "I'm stuck!" – and he was.

"Back, Thomas, back!" called his driver. Thomas tried to go back but his wheels spun round and he couldn't move. More snow fell down and piled up around him.

The guard went back for help while the driver, fireman and passengers tried to dig the snow away from Thomas's wheels. But as fast as they dug, more snow slipped down and Thomas was nearly buried.

"Oh! My wheels and coupling rods!" said Thomas. "I shall have to stop here until I'm frozen. What a silly engine I am." And Thomas began to cry.

At last a bus came to rescue all the passengers. Then Terence the tractor came chugging through the tunnel.

Snow never worried him.

He pulled the empty coaches away and came back for Thomas.

Thomas's wheels were clear but they still spun round and round when he tried to move. Terence tugged and slipped, and slipped and tugged.

At last he pulled Thomas clear of the snow, ready for the journey home.

"Thank you, Terence, your caterpillars are *splendid*," said Thomas, gratefully.

"I hope that you will be sensible now, Thomas," said his driver, crossly.

"I'll try," said Thomas, as he puffed home.

THOMAS

EDWARD

GORDON